SOUNDBITES

Keyboards

Roger Thomas

www.heinemann.co.uk/library
Visit our website to find out more information about Heinemann Library books.

To order:
☎ Phone 44 (0) 1865 888066
▤ Send a fax to 44 (0) 1865 314091
▯ Visit the Heinemann Bookshop at www.heinemann.co.uk/library to browse our catalogue and order online.

First published in Great Britain by Heinemann Library, Halley Court, Jordan Hill, Oxford, OX2 8EJ, a division of Reed Educational and Professional Publishing Ltd.
Heinemann is a registered trademark of Reed Educational and Professional Publishing Ltd.

OXFORD MELBOURNE AUCKLAND
JOHANNESBURG BLANTYRE GABORONE
IBADAN PORTSMOUTH NH (USA) CHICAGO

Designed by Paul Davies and Associates
Originated by Ambassador Litho Ltd.
Printed at Wing King Tong in Hong Kong

ISBN 0 431 13074 4 (hardback)   ISBN 0 431 13081 7 (paperback)
06 05 04 03 02   06 05 04 03 02
10 9 8 7 6 5 4 3 2   10 9 8 7 6 5 4 3 2 1

British Library Cataloguing in Publication Data

Thomas, Roger, 1956-
  Keyboards. - (Soundbites)
  1.Keyboard instruments - Juvenile literature 2.Keyboard
  music - Juvenile literature
  I.Title
  786.8

Acknowledgements
The Publishers would like to thank the following for permission to reproduce photographs: Corbis: Pg.15; Eyewire: Pg.12; Hulton: Pg.22; Jazz Index: Pg.5, Pg.20; Lebrecht Picture Library: Pg.4, Pg.6, Pg.9, Pg.11, Pg.16, Pg.18, Pg.19, Pg.21; Mary Evans Picture Library: Pg.13, Pg.14; Redferns: Pg.10, Pg.26; Redferns/Outline: Pg.23; Unknown: Pg.17, Pg.24, Pg.29; Yamaha: Pg.27, Pg.28.

Cover photograph reproduced with permission of Photodisc.

Our thanks to Brian Shea for his comments in the preparation of this book.

Every effort has been made to contact copyright holders of any material reproduced in this book. Any omissions will be rectified in subsequent printings if notice is given to the publishers.

Contents

Any words appearing in bold, **like this**, are explained in the Glossary

Introduction

Today the instrumental keyboard is one of the first images that comes to mind when we think of music. The sequence of white keys overlaid with groups of two and three black keys is a strong visual reminder of how music seems to 'work'. The notes go from left to right, from the lowest to the highest, which seems, in the **West**, entirely logical. The difference between any two **adjacent** notes seems to be consistent. At any point on the keyboard, the distance between one note and another one that somehow sounds the same, only higher (the **octave**), is constant.

A spread of notes

A left-to-right or low-to-high layout of notes is seen in many-stringed instruments, such as the **zither**, as well as in the tuned **percussion** instruments of many cultures, including Africa (the balafon), Java and Bali (gamelan instruments) and the West (orchestral tuned percussion). In combination with the development of mechanical keys, this concept was the forerunner of the modern keyboard.

A left-to-right note layout is found on many different types of instrument in many cultures.

Origins

One theory proposes that the keyboard was the idea of an Italian Benedictine monk named Guido d'Arezzo (c.990–1050) who also made important contributions to the theory and **notation** of music. Another suggests that it was developed from the **hurdy-gurdy**, a stringed instrument that has buttons for holding the strings down at various points to change the notes. However, a keyboard is essentially a system of levers, and the idea of using this technique to control a musical instrument pre-dates both d'Arezzo and the hurdy-gurdy.

The hydraulis

The hydraulis may have been the first true keyboard instrument. It was invented by an engineer named Ctesibios in the ancient city of Alexandria in about 250 BCE. It was essentially a pipe organ (see pages 16–17), as the sound of the instrument came from flute-like tubes. Air was pushed into the instrument with hand pumps. However, Ctesibios devised a system that allowed a reserve air supply to build up inside the instrument. This was regulated by water, which would flow into the system to keep the air pressure constant even if the air was not pumped in with a constant rhythm. Early illustrations show that the hydraulis either had large keys, played with the palm of the hand, or **sliders** that were moved in order to let air into the pipes. This simple idea was used again in organ design centuries later.

This is a 4th century drawing of a hydraulis.

Types of keyboard instrument

Today, it is usual (and perfectly sensible) to refer to keyboard instruments as a group because, as well as sharing the distinctive layout of keys that became the standard design by the middle of the 15th century, the basic method of playing all keyboard instruments is the same. That said, the differences in how the various instruments respond when their keys are pressed means that many variations in technique are needed to be a proficient 'multi-keyboardist'.

The musicologists' method

An early system of classifying musical instruments was published in 1914 by two famous **musicologists** named Erich von Hornbostel and Curt Sachs. This system classifies instruments according to how they make sound – whether by using strings (**chordophones**), wind (**aerophones**), materials that naturally have a musical sound when struck, scraped, shaken or rubbed (**idiophones**), drums and related instruments (**membranophones**) and mechanical and electrical instruments.

The interior of a piano clearly shows how it relies on mechanical design.

Keyboard groups

As different keyboard instruments make sounds in different ways (old cinema organs can even include real drums), it is possible to sub-divide the keyboard family into groups:

- STRINGS: the piano, which makes sound using a system of strings that are struck by felt-covered **hammers**; the harpsichord family, which have strings that are plucked by a mechanical system; the clavichord family, which has strings that are struck by light metal hammers.

- WIND: the pipe organ and the reed organ or harmonium work by having air blown through pipes or across metal **reeds**.

- IDIOPHONIC KEYBOARD INSTRUMENTS: the celeste, which has keyboard-controlled hammers that strike metal bars; the original type of electric piano, which is similar except that the sound comes from thin metal tongues, with the sound being **amplified** via **pickups** on the same principle as the electric guitar

- ELECTRO-MECHANICAL INSTRUMENTS: the type of electric piano described above also belongs in this category, as does the **Clavinet** and the original type of electric organ, which produces sounds using motorized metal discs that spin in **magnetic** fields to produce electronic **tones**. This category also includes the Mellotron, an electric keyboard instrument, which plays back a sound pre-recorded on a length of tape every time a key is pressed.

- ELECTRONIC INSTRUMENTS: these can be distinguished from all other keyboard instruments in that they contain no moving parts other than the keys themselves, which simply act as switches to activate electronic circuits.

How keyboards work

Although all keyboards have an identical layout (with the exception of a very few experimental designs), the sequence of actions that are set into motion when a key is pressed differs completely in the case of each type of instrument. The only other thing all keyboard instruments have in common is some sort of casing that encloses the instrument. On **acoustic** instruments, such as the piano, this will contribute to the instrument's sound as well as protecting its **components**.

The basic piano

Each key on the piano activates a series of wooden levers that carry out a sequence of actions. Firstly, a felt **hammer** is 'flicked' so that it hits a set of strings. This produces the note. The hammer is then immediately lifted off the strings, so that its full sound will be heard. At the same time a **damper** that normally rests on the string is lifted away. These dampers prevent the strings from taking on **resonant** 'echoes' from other notes. When the key is released, the hammer and dampers return to their original positions. A piano also has two or three pedals which, by damping and un-damping the strings, change the instrument's **tone** by making the sound 'brighter' or 'softer'.

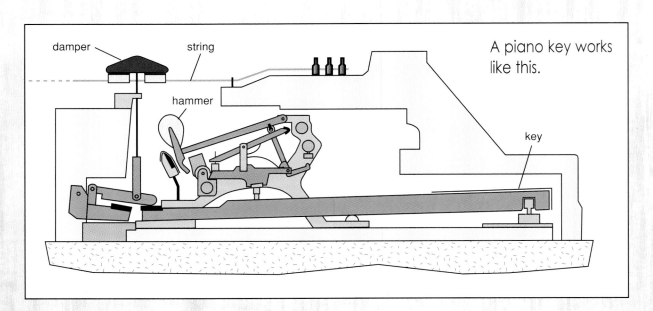

damper string hammer key

A piano key works like this.

The harpsichord family

This group of instruments includes the harpsichord, together with the spinet and the virginal, which are smaller instruments with a similar mechanism. On these instruments, each key presses a small tab against a string, which plucks it in the same way as a **plectrum** can be used to pluck the strings of a guitar.

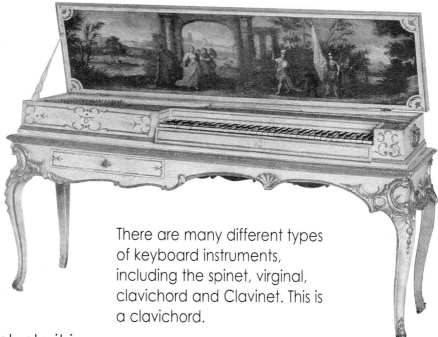

There are many different types of keyboard instruments, including the spinet, virginal, clavichord and Clavinet. This is a clavichord.

The clavichord

On this type of instrument, the keys cause thin metal hammers to strike metal strings inside the instrument.

Pipe and reed organs

The key mechanism on these instruments is attached to a device which pumps air through a system of **valves**. This allows air to blow into flute-like pipes or across thin metal **reeds** to produce sounds.

Electro-mechanical instruments

This family includes the original type of electric piano and the **Clavinet**, which is essentially a large **amplified** clavichord. In each case, the keys are mechanical, causing some form of hammer or striker to make contact with a small plate, bar or tongue. The sound is then amplified electronically.

Electronic instruments

Sound-producing electronic circuits come in many designs, and different electronic keyboards may use one or several of these. However, in every case, the key mechanism is simply a switch, which allows **electric currents** to pass into the instrument.

The piano

Why the piano was invented

The piano is one of the most widely recognized instruments in the world today, yet it is a comparatively recent invention. Around the middle of the 18th century, changing trends in **composition** meant that more emphasis was being placed on the expressive power of music. Most keyboard music was played on the harpsichord, which worked using plucked strings. The instrument's **tone** was impossible to change and it was unable to produce varied **dynamics**. Harpsichord makers tried to improve the instrument by using **shutters** and **dampers** and by adding a second keyboard with extra strings, or that plucked the strings in different places to give different tones. However, it was clear that a completely new instrument was needed.

Cristofori and Silbermann

The idea of the piano, however, had actually begun during the previous century. Two instrument builders were largely responsible for the design of the piano as we now know it. The first was Bartolomeo Cristofori, who lived in Italy during the late 17th century. He first devised an instrument called the *arpicimbalo*. This was based on the dulcimer, which was a stringed instrument played by hand using **hammers**.

This square dates from 1817.

Crisotfori added a key mechanism to this instrument, then went on to build a group of instruments with soft mechanical hammers and keyboards, which he called *gravicembali col piano e forte* (harpsichords with soft and loud sounds). The strings were hammered and the loudness of the instrument could be changed by how hard it was played. This resulted in the name *fortepiano* (the name still used today for pianos of a very early design) and the more familiar *pianoforte* (soft and loud). This is now the (rarely used) full name of the piano. A German organ-builder, Gottfried Silbermann (1683–1753), then improved on this design and, by the early 1800s, composers such as Beethoven (1770–1827) were using pianos similar to those today.

Shapes and sizes

The piano became very popular, and instruments were made in many styles for use in different settings. The following are some examples of the different designs:

The concert grand is the largest type of grand piano.

- THE GRAND PIANO has a distinctive wing-like shape that matches the lengths of the strings inside, from low-**pitched** (long and thick) to high-pitched (shorter and thinner).

- THE UPRIGHT PIANO is designed in a space-saving vertical case. This makes it the most popular piano for use at home, in classrooms or wherever space is restricted. Early types of upright piano kept the wing-like shape of the grand piano, leading to designs known as the pyramid piano, the harp piano (which had exposed strings like a harp) and even the giraffe piano.

- HISTORICAL PIANOS, such as the fortepiano and square piano are still found today, as many pianists like to play early piano music on the exact instrument the composer would have heard it on.

The harpsichord family

The harpsichord preceded the piano as the most widely used keyboard instrument for concert music. A great deal of the music that we think of today as piano music, such as the 'Goldberg Variations' by Johann Sebastian Bach (1685–1750) were in fact originally written for the harpsichord and organs.

Early harpsichords

The first successful harpischords were made in Italy in the 1500s, although instrument makers had been experimenting with the basic principles of the instrument for two hundred years before. The harpsichord is made of various kinds of wood and has metal strings. Spinets and virginals are smaller instruments that work in the same way.

Later variations

The sound of the harpsichord is limited by its action. The notes cannot be **sustained**, as they can on a piano (by raising the **dampers**) or on a wind or **bowed** string instrument, because the plucking of a string produces a short sound. Also, whenever a note is played, the mechanism must work with enough force to make the string 'twang' cleanly, which restricts the instrument's volume. This was

Early harpsichords were small and had thick and heavy cases. Later versions, like this one, however, had lighter casework and were highly decorative.

noted by the 18th-century composer Couperin, who wrote in 1713 that he would be grateful to anyone who could 'contrive to render this instrument capable of expression'.

It was not until the invention of the piano (see pages 10–11) that these problems would truly be resolved. In the meantime, harpsichord builders worked hard to think of ways of improving their instruments. One method was by adding a second keyboard with more strings, with the mechanisms of the two keyboards plucking the strings at different points along their lengths. A string plucked in the middle has a rich, round **tone**, while a string plucked nearer the end has a hard, bright tone. Interesting effects could be obtained by playing the two keyboards at once, or by 'echoing' notes on one with notes on the other. Extra sets of strings

The spinet is a smaller, harpsichord-like instrument and therefore more suitable to home use than the harpsichord itself.

could be 'switched on' by moving levers called 'stops' (named after organ **stops** – see pages 16–17). These could be operated by hand or with pedals. Harpsichords continued to be made after the invention of the piano, so there can be no doubt that harpsichord makers felt the need to keep improving in order to compete with this new instrument.

Playing techniques

Harpsichord players themselves also thought of ways of overcoming the shortcomings of the instrument, often by using creative playing techniques that would deceive the ear of the listener. These included playing quickly or slowly to give the impression that the music was louder or quieter and using trills (two adjacent notes played very quickly one after the other) to imply a single sustained note.

The clavichord

The clavichord is a very old instrument that may have been developed from a very early, simple instrument called the **monochord**, which consisted of a single string, a **soundbox** and a movable **bridge**. However, this simple keyboard instrument had a very interesting history.

Internal workings

The keys of a clavichord are pivoted in the middle. When a key is pressed, the opposite end rises up like a seesaw. The end of the key has a blunt metal blade on it, called a **tangent**. Strings are stretched across the interior of the instrument so that each blade strikes a pair of strings (tuned to the same note) when the key is pressed. When the key is released, the tangent falls away. On simpler types, there are fewer strings and each tangent strikes them in a different place. This gives a range of notes from one string.

Some clavichords are fairly large...

Strictly domestic

The sound of the clavichord is quiet and delicate. For this reason it was mainly used in the home, until the piano and harpsicord became the usual home keyboard instruments in the 18th century. In that sense, it was the ancestor of today's electronic home keyboard. However, clavichords are still made today. While their main use is by specialist keyboard players to play period music, one manufacturer has promoted the clavichord as the ideal non-electronic instrument for music students, because the smallest types are very light and portable and also won't disturb the neighbours!

A sensitive instrument

The clavichord was valued for the subtle ways in which its sound could be changed, unlike the harpsichord (see pages 12–13). Its simple action meant that the loudness of the sound could be controlled by simply striking the keys harder. Pressing the keys down would make the note higher by stretching the strings with the tangent. Wobbling the key from side to side created a subtle **vibrato** effect, like that used by violinists.

Smaller table-top clavichords were popular for use in the home in the 17th and 18th centuries.

Organ practice

One type of clavichord, made in the mid-18th century, had a set of pedals laid out like a second keyboard and attached to strong vertical wires. When the pedals were pressed, the wires would operate a second mechanism, underneath the main one. This type required a hands-and-feet technique like that used on a pipe organ, so organists used it at home as a practice instrument.

The pipe organ

A type of pipe organ seems to have been the very first keyboard instrument of all (see page 4). Over the centuries, the instrument has developed enormously. However, the principle of its operation has remained constant. Air is pumped through a set of flute-like pipes, with the sound of the instrument being changed by diverting the air into different pipes using a set of **valves** called **stops**. Pipe organs were originally powered by hand- or foot-operated **bellows**, but modern instruments have electric pumps.

Church organs

The pipe organ is mainly associated with churches, where the instrument had become popular by the 15th century. These instruments were built into the buildings, because of their enormous size, and design preferences varied from region to region. For example the Rhineland area of what is now Germany boasted some of the most technically advanced organs, with two or three separate keyboards (known as **manuals**), whereas Italian and French organs were simpler, with a single manual and a small range of **stops**. English organ-builders were particularly interested in creating a wider variety of sounds for the instrument, experimenting with **reed stops**, which sent the air into pipes that also contained **reeds** (see pages 18–19). However, English organ design suffered a setback in the 17th century. The church decided that the loud noise was offensive to God and many church organs were destroyed.

This is an early Baroque pipe organ at Guimiliau Church in Germany.

Theatre organs

Organs were first installed in theatres and cinema buildings in the early 20th century. They were used to provide musical accompaniments – for example for silent films – and for playing musical interludes between on-stage performances. They would also be installed in other places of entertainment,

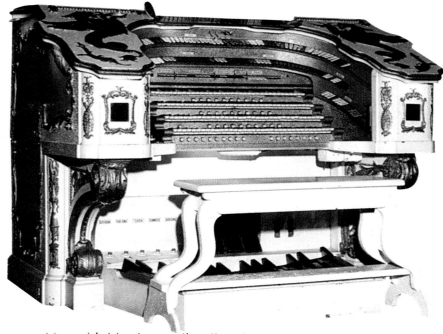

Many highly-decorative theatre organs have been preserved by enthusiasts and are still played in performances today.

such as ice rinks. Again, their working principles were the same as for other pipe organs, but they differed in the way they were 'voiced' in terms of how the pipes sounded. Because they were associated with recreation, they would often have a warm, 'jolly' **tone**. The cheery sound of the theatre organ often included sound effects made by **percussion** instruments, which were built into the organ's mechanism.

Concert organs

Because the pipe organ is capable of producing a very powerful, varied and expressive sound, instruments were also built into concert halls and theatres. Concert hall instruments were similar to church organs in design, although they would often be very large in order to accommodate the wide variety of music played on them. This includes **solo** organ recitals, concertos, where the organ plays with an orchestra, or masses and **oratorios**. These works often require an organ, an orchestra, a choir and vocal soloists. The largest organ in the world is a concert hall organ in the Municipal Auditorium in Atlantic City in the USA. It has 33,112 pipes; 1928 stops and a total of 12 manuals.

Reed organs

Because of the way in which **reed** organs produce sounds (by forcing air over metal reeds which then vibrate), this family of keyboard instruments is related to two other families that are played in quite different ways. One is the group of wind instruments that includes the Chinese sheng and the Western harmonium and melodica, which were developed from it. The other is the group of **bellows**-operated metal reed instruments that include the accordion, melodeon and concertina. Of these, the free-**bass** accordion is perhaps the closest relative to the reed organ. It is so-called because it has a keyboard at each end that allows the player a free choice of bass notes, instead of using the fixed **chords** produced by buttons. It could be thought of as a reed organ split in half and played sideways.

The compact Western harmoniums were often used overseas by Christian missionaries to accompany hymns.

The Western harmonium

Because some models are designed to look like pipe organs (often to the extent of having false pipes attached, this instrument is often thought of as being many centuries old. In fact, it was **patented** in Paris by an instrument designer named Debain as recently as 1848. The name 'harmonium' became used for reed organs in general. One of the main functions of the harmonium was as a substitute for the pipe organ. In addition, while early pipe organs could be quite small, by the mid-19th century most organs were larger and installed in buildings. The harmonium was much lighter and smaller and could be transported fairly easily. This meant that they could be supplied to small country churches where pipe organs were not practical.

A cheap keyboard

Before relatively cheap electronic keyboards were available, a simple form of electric harmonium for home use was for sale in high street shops. Known as the electric chord organ, it had an air pump operated by mains electricity (or sometimes batteries), a set of chord buttons like an accordion, and a keyboard.

The harmonium is often used at Indian celebrations and festivals.

The harmonium in India

The harmonium is also used extensively in Indian music. The instrument usually used is a small type, which is rested directly on the floor or on a suitable surface, or carried by the player with a strap. The keyboard, which is laid out like a **Western** keyboard, is played with one hand, while the player uses the other hand to pump a small set of bellows at the back of the instrument. Because the instrument is small, the air has only a short distance to travel between the bellows and the reeds. This, combined with the fact that the action of the bellows is very direct and can be controlled by the player, gives the Indian harmonium a lively, agile sound.

Electro-mechanical and early electronic keyboards

Experiments in producing musical sound electronically began at the end of the 19th century and, before long, many inventors were producing designs that added new dimensions to the music of the time. The traditional keyboard layout could easily be adapted for use as a set of switches, so the link between electronics and keyboard instruments was established at an early stage.

The Ondes Martenot

The 'Ondes' was **patented** in 1922 by the French inventor Maurice Martenot. It works by using electronic **oscillators**, which produce very pure musical **tones**. The player controls these from the instrument's five-**octave** keyboard and by sliding a finger along a wire set below the keyboard. This allowed the instrument to produce piping, birdsong-like notes and swooping **glissandi**, which sound quite unique, even in comparison with modern digital instruments. Because the instrument has such a distinctive tone, it is still being made and played today.

The Ondes Martenot is perhaps the best example of an early electronic keyboard still in regular use.

The electric organ

This instrument was the forerunner of the enormous variety of electronic keyboard instruments in use today. However, the original type, invented in 1935 by an American named Laurens Hammond, was in fact an **electro-mechanical** instrument, as it used motorized discs called **tonewheels**, which spun in a **magnetic** field to produce an **electric current**. This in turn was adapted to produce musical notes that could be modified by **sliders** (called 'drawbars'), which changed the tone. Hammond originally intended the instrument to be used as a substitute for the pipe organ, both in religious settings and at home. However, its sounds, which had a distinctive 'warble' (known as **vibrato**), and which could be varied from smooth and mellow to sharp and penetrating were to prove a great success with rock and jazz musicians. Unlike modern **digital** instruments, the Hammond organ has a slightly inconsistent sound, which gives it a 'feel' more like that of an **acoustic** instrument. For this reason, classic Hammonds are still sought after by musicians today. Several other manufacturers also made electric organs.

The Hammond organ has an instantly recognizable sound.

The electric piano and Clavinet

The original electric piano was also an electro-mechanical instrument. It was invented by an American named Harold Rhodes in the late 1940s. Rhodes's design used a keyboard that caused **hammers** to strike small metal plates inside the instrument. The sound was then **amplified** electronically. Rhodes had developed his invention from simple, homemade instruments, which he had been using as **occupational therapy** for wounded American airmen. Again, this instrument had a smooth, bell-like sound that is still sought after by rock and jazz musicians today. Other manufacturers also made electric pianos, with one also producing the **Clavinet** – a type of large, amplified clavichord with a cutting, 'funky' sound.

21

Early synthesizers

All instruments could be said to be 'synthesizers' in that they create sounds which do not exist in the natural world, but which are 'synthetic'. However, all conventional instruments have their own natural sound and, for centuries, musicians and philosophers had been wondering if it would ever be possible to assemble any sound from its most basic **components**. The story of the synthesizer, an instrument that produces sounds purely electronically, is essentially the story of this idea. The earliest synthesizers were quite distinct from **electro-mechanical** instruments such as the Hammond organ and the electric piano, which produced a specific type of sound.

The RCA Synthesizer had a 'typewriter' keyboard.

The first synthesizer

The earliest experiments with sounds other than those produced by conventional instruments involved the use of sound recordings. Various techniques were used, such as recording the sounds of 'non-instruments' like pots and pans and cutting and re-joining recording tape so that sounds changed unexpectedly. However, this was both time-consuming and 'artificial', in that the results could only exist as a final recording and not as a live performance. This situation began to change with the invention in the USA of the first electronic synthesizer, the RCA Electronic Music Synthesizer, in 1955 at the Sarnoff Research Centre, New Jersey. However, this was a large, bulky instrument that had to be programmed using a roll of punched paper. Again, live performance was not possible. It did, however, have a 'keyboard' of a sort, although this was just a typewriter-like keyboard for punching holes in the paper roll.

Robert Moog's innovations

It was not until 1964 that synthesizers became widely available. The most important development was the invention of a system called 'voltage control' by synthesizer pioneer Robert Moog. The type of electronic **synthesis** used at the time involved electronic sound-producing circuits called **oscillators**, which had to be individually tuned to the note chosen by the user. Moog invented a method of controlling the **pitch** of an oscillator using electrical power and standardized the amount of power needed at one volt per **octave**. This meant that a given amount of power would produce the chosen note just by switching the power on. This system was ideally suited to keyboard control, as a keyboard-shaped row of switches was easy to make. It was only at this point that the synthesizer became a keyboard instrument. Even then, synthesizers without keyboards continued to be produced.

Synthesis to go

Having established the basic design of the keyboard-controlled synthesizer, Moog then worked on refining the practical aspects of what was still a rather bulky instrument. This resulted in the launch of the Mini-Moog in 1970. This was a fully portable, self-contained synthesizer, controlled by a built-in keyboard. Its design allowed it to be used onstage by rock bands, alongside other keyboards such as the electric organ and electric piano.

The Mini-Moog was the first portable keyboard synthesizer.

Polyphonic synthesizers, samplers and workstations

These developments are the three most significant advances in electronic keyboard technology since the first commercially available keyboard synthesizers were produced in the 1960s. Each innovation added a new dimension to the playing of electronic keyboards.

The need for polyphonic synthesis

After Robert Moog had perfected the portable keyboard synthesizer, the next problem to be solved was that of **polyphony**, or the ability of a synthesizer to play more than one note at a time. Both the Mini-Moog (see page 23) and other similar instruments were limited to playing single notes. This was unlike conventional keyboard instruments, and even the earlier electric organ and electric piano did not have this shortcoming. In the short term, this led to two developments. Firstly, rock keyboard players usually added a synthesizer to their pre-existing organ/piano set-up rather than using a synthesizer on its own. Secondly, synthesizer players had to develop various techniques to disguise the **monophonic** (single note) nature of their instruments. These included playing very fast **arpeggios** that gave the impression of **chords** and playing two instruments simultaneously.

The first 'polysynths'

With the invention of the microchip, it became possible to make much smaller electronic circuits. This allowed Robert Moog's company to produce the first satisfactory polyphonic synthesizer, the PolyMoog, in 1978. Effectively, the instrument had the most important circuits duplicated on a separate chip for each key. However, since each key had to be programmed individually, the range of sounds it produced was limited. Shortly afterwards, another company launched a synthesizer called the Prophet 5 which solved this problem by 'memorizing' control settings for different sounds.

Digital technology now allows all the necessary information to produce polyphonic sound to be stored in the instrument as computer data.

Keyboard samplers

Keyboard instruments that can play back pre-recorded sounds date back to a 1960s instrument called the Mellotron, which used pre-recorded tape. However, in 1979 an instrument called the Fairlight CMI (computer musical instrument) was launched, which was also able to '**sample**' any sound by making a **digital** recording of it and converting it into a musical **scale**. It was manufactured until 1988, but was bulky and very expensive – the final version cost up to $175,000 – and sampling soon became a common feature of much smaller, cheaper keyboards, either as an active process or as a means of supplying the instrument with pre-loaded sounds.

The music workstation

Together with polyphony and sampling, the invention of **sequencing** – the ability of an instrument to memorize a series of notes and replay them as required – made it possible for the keyboard player to create and record entire multi-part **compositions** on a single instrument.

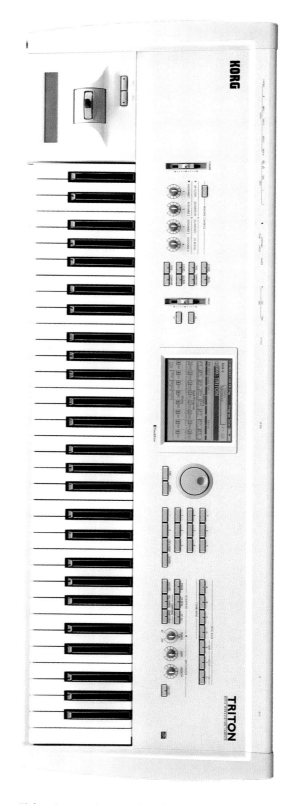

This cheap home keyboard has a built-in sequencer.

Computers, keyboards and music

The technology used in computers and in keyboard instruments allows them to 'talk' to each other in many ways.

Early experiments

Computers were first used to make music without necessarily involving keyboards. Early computer-generated music often used computers to 'translate' mathematical data into sound information, such as the 1970 composition by Charles Dodge called 'Earth's Magnetic Field'. Alternatively, the computer would 'write' a composition for conventional instruments based on random numbers or a mathematical system. However, the development in the 1980s of a computer language called MIDI (musical instrument digital interface) allowed keyboards and computers to work together.

Computers like this one can be accessed from a keyboard using a MIDI connection.

What MIDI does

MIDI allows electronic musical instruments to transmit and receive musical information in the form of computer data. This can be what notes to play, in what order, at what **tempo**, at what volume, how long the notes should be and so on. This allows, for example, one electronic keyboard to play the sounds of another, or a keyboard that may have no built-in sounds to play the sounds of any number of keyboardless 'sound modules'. These instruments contain the means to produce sounds, but no 'built-in' way of playing them. This gives the player a massive choice of sounds, all of which can be controlled from one keyboard if required. MIDI also allows music to be stored as data **sequences**, which can then be played back, edited and so on, either using a computer or a smaller unit known as a sequencer.

MIDI, keyboards and computers

Even most ordinary home PCs now have some music-making capability. With a MIDI connection to a computer, the user can:

- use a keyboard to play the sounds in the PC's soundcard – the circuit supplied with most PCs for producing sound
- record a musical performance using a keyboard and edit it using one of the many software packages available for this purpose
- store the performance on disk and replay it elsewhere.

Computers and sound editing

The computer can help the electronic keyboard player in many other ways. One example is by the use of a type of software called a patch editor. Early synthesizers such as the Mini-Moog (see pages 22–23) were covered in knobs and switches for changing the sound. Later synthesizers had more sophisticated sounds, but often had to be programmed by using fiddly, multi-function buttons and layers of tiny menus displayed on a small LCD screen on the instrument. However, patch editor software 'unfolds' all this information onto a computer screen. The user can then see all the ways in which the sound can be changed, adjust them with mouse clicks and send the results to the keyboard via MIDI. This has become increasingly important with the increase in the complexity of electronic keyboard instruments.

This sequencer
can be programmed
by keyboard-like buttons
and can store musical 'phrases'.

27

Keyboards and the future

Keyboard instruments have had a central role in **Western** music for centuries. Today, most forms of music from this whole period are being

The Yamaha DJX keyboard is 'DJ-friendly'.

preserved, performed and recorded somewhere in the world, which means that there is a continued demand for appropriate keyboard instruments for each style. It is unlikely, therefore, that any individual type of keyboard instrument is going to disappear. Moreover, manufacturers are spending a great deal of time and effort in keeping up with demand.

Classical music

The piano, organ, harpsichord and other keyboard instruments generally associated with classical music remain in huge demand, although this can range from a lot (the piano) to rather less (the clavichord). However, while the piano is popular and will be made in specialist factories for the foreseeable future, other instruments are generally handmade by individual craftspeople or assembled from kit form.

Occasionally, **digital** technology is used in classical performance, such as when an amateur orchestra, for example, uses an electronic keyboard (playing an appropriate sound) as a substitute for a harpsichord, because the cost of hiring and tuning a 'real' harpsichord can be large. However, **acoustic** keyboard instruments will never be completely replaced by electronic substitutes, because electronic instruments need to be played through an amplifier and loud speakers. This has a fundamental effect on the sound, making it quite unlike that of a 'natural' instrument.

Rock, pop and dance music

With so many styles of music being created (and recreated) in this field, demand for all types of keyboard instrument will probably remain considerable and is likely to increase. The following are a few examples:

- **HYBRID** INSTRUMENTS, such as the Yamaha DJX keyboard, are a new development. This particular example combines a keyboard with the digital equivalent of 'scratch mixing' facilities used by DJs.
- 'RETRO' KEYBOARDS (e.g. the Hammond organ), manufactured in the early days of electronic keyboards, are in great demand, so there will probably be further developments in re-creating their sounds on modern keyboards.
- 'SOFT-SYNTH' KEYBOARDS are a particularly interesting area. In an attempt to make keyboard sounds available at the lowest possible cost, some companies are producing 'keyboard instruments', which exist only as software. When loaded into a computer (see pages 26–27), the software simulates the sounds of the instrument in question, and displays an interactive image of it on the screen, complete with an image of the keyboard layout. This can then be operated via a **sequencer** or **controller keyboard** (see pages 26 and 27), or 'played' on-screen by clicking the 'keys' using a mouse.

A 'soft' keyboard – complete with virtual coffee stains – on a computer screen.

Glossary

acoustic relating to sound – when used to describe an instrument, it usually means 'without electronics'

adjacent next to each other

aerophones instruments which produce sound by using wind

amplify to make louder

arpeggios groups of notes in which the notes are sounded individually in sequence

bass the lowest range of notes in normal use

bellows a folded box-like pouch, usually made of leather, which is used to pump air into instruments such as reed and pipe organs

bowed played with a bow (a stick with a length of hair attached)

bridge a sharp vertical edge on a stringed instrument, over which the strings are stretched

chordophones instruments which produce sound using vibrating strings

chords groups of notes sounded simultaneously

Clavinet an electro-mechanical instrument which works like a clavichord but with the sound being amplified electronically

components parts

composition a piece of written music

controller keyboard an electronic keyboard which produces no sound itself but is used to access sounds stored in another electronic instrument or in a computer

damper a device which mutes or muffles the sound of an instrument

digital using a computer-like 'language' of ones and zeros to store information – also used to describe synthesizers which work in this way

dynamics the loudness or softness of a sound

electric current the passage of electricity through conductive material

electro-mechanical describes instruments which use a mixture of mechanical and electrical means to make sounds

glissandi sounds made by 'sliding' from one note to another

hammer the part of the keyboard mechanism that hits the strings

hurdy-gurdy a stringed instrument operated by a handle which rubs a rosin-covered wheel against the strings

hybrid a cross between two types

idiophones percussion instruments which produce sounds from hard surfaces, such as gongs or woodblocks, as opposed to membranophones

magnetic involving magnets or magnetism

manuals the keyboards on an organ or harpsichord, so-called to distinguish them from pedals

membranophones instruments such as drums which make a sound with a vibrating membrane

monochord an early instrument with a single string

monophonic able to produce only one note at a time

musicologist someone who studies aspects of music such as the history of music or its cultural role

notation a system of writing down music

occupational therapy constructive tasks given to victims of illness or injury to aid in their rehabilitation

octave eight consecutive whole notes

oratorio a dramatic, usually religious musical work for orchestra and voices

oscillators electronic circuits which produce an output which can be heard as a musical note

patented licensed as the inventor's original design by the government

percussion instruments played by striking (or, in a few cases, friction)

pickup an electronic device attached to an instrument which allows it to be amplified electronically

pitch how high or low a note is

plectrum used for plucking the strings on a stringed instrument

polyphony several notes at once

reed a strip of cane, which vibrates when air is blown across it

reed stops stops on an organ which allow air to pass through pipes which contain reeds

resonant describes something which vibrates when exposed to sound

sample a short digital sound recording stored in the memory of a computer or electronic instrument

scale an arrangement of notes in ascending or descending order of pitch

sequence a specific order of events (such as musical notes); to place events in order

shutters doors which close off a space

sliders devices on early organs which were slid in and out to divert air into specific pipes

solo a section or piece of music featuring a single performer, or one performer alone

soundbox a hollow object or structure used to amplify the sound of an instrument

stops hand-operated valves on reed and pipe organs which allow air into particular pipes (also used for mechanical controls on harpsichords)

sustain to keep something (a note) going over a long time

synthesis making or constructing something out of individual parts

tangent one of the small metal hammers which strikes the strings of a clavichord

tempo the speed at which a piece of music is played

tone the quality of a sound, often described in visual terms - bright, dark, thin etc.

tonewheels metal discs used in 'classic' electronic organs – they produce sound by spinning in a magnetic field

valves devices which regulate the flow of something (e.g. air in a wind instrument, electric current in an electronic organ)

vibrato a continuous variation in the pitch of a note

West/ern this terms usually used by musicologists to refer to mainland Europe and the English-speaking countries

zither a box-shaped instrument with strings which are plucked or strummed

Index

Titles in the *Soundbites* series include:

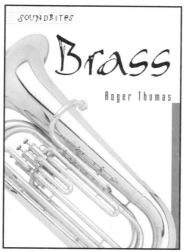

Hardback   0 431 13070 1

Hardback   0 431 13071 X

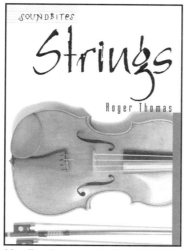

Hardback   0 431 13072 8

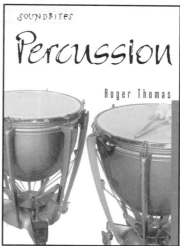

Hardback   0 431 13073 6

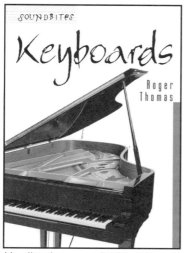

Hardback   0 431 13074 4

Hardback   0 431 13075 2

Find out about the other titles in this series on our website www.heinemann.co.uk/library